TOUGH GUIDES

HOW TO SURVIVE ON A
DESERT ISLAND

JIM PIPE

PowerKiDS
press.

New York

Published in 2013 by The Rosen Publishing Group, Inc.
29 East 21st Street, New York, NY 10010

Produced for Rosen by Calcium Creative Ltd
Editors for Calcium Creative Ltd: Sarah Eason and Jennifer Sanderson
US Editor: Sara Antill
Designer: Simon Borrough

Photo Credits: Cover: Shutterstock: Eduard Kyslynskyy, Vlad Ghiea. Inside: Steve F-E Cameron
(Merlin-UK) 27tl; Shutterstock: Annetje 5tl, ArtTomCat 4c, Brocreative 24c, Kris Butler 13t,
Jakub Cejpek 11c, Bobby Deal/RealDealPhoto 17tl, Dirk Ercken 10br, EcoPrint 22cl, FotoVeto
19t, Paolo Gianti 4l, 16l, lkunl 25t, Iakov Kalinin 23t, Intraclique LLC 15c, Xavier Marchant 6l, 18l,
Mayskyphoto 29t, Movit 8l, 20l, Tyler Olson 8cl, PhotoHappiness 4cr, Pinosub 6c, Leigh Prather
26cl, Daniel Rajszczak 16c, Valery Shanin 28cl, Szefei 7c, Aleksandar Todorovic 18cl, Graham
Tomlin 14c, Andrij Vatsyk 9t, Dani Vincek 12l, 24l, Vladoskan 14l, 26l, VVO 10l, 22l, Marty Wakat
21c, Richard Waters 20c, David Wingate 12c.

Library of Congress Cataloging-in-Publication Data

Pipe, Jim, 1966–
 How to survive on a desert island / by Jim Pipe.
    p. cm. — (Tough guides)
 Includes index.
 ISBN 978-1-4488-7870-3 (library binding) — ISBN 978-1-4488-7935-9 (pbk.) —
ISBN 978-1-4488-7941-0 (6-pack)
 1. Desert survival—Juvenile literature. I. Title.
 GV200.5.P379 2013
 613.6′9—dc23
                                        2011052894

Manufactured in the United States of America

CPSIA Compliance Information: Batch #SW12PK: For Further Information contact Rosen Publishing, New York, New York at 1-800-237-9932

Contents

SURVIVAL!

Thanks to modern technology, our world is getting smaller. We can fly over a giant ocean in a few hours. Yet many parts of our planet are still wild and dangerous. A fierce storm can still send a ship crashing into the rocks. A faulty engine can force an airplane to land in the ocean.

Pacific Ocean

PACIFIC OCEAN
WHERE: stretches from Australia and Asia to the Americas
AREA: 64.1 million square miles (166 million km²)

Imagine surviving a plane crash or **shipwreck**. You struggle ashore, only to find yourself all alone on an island. You are in the middle of the Pacific Ocean, thousands of miles (km) from the nearest town. Suddenly, the world seems very, very big. Could you survive? How might you be rescued?

I SURVIVED

In 1722, sailor Philip Ashton hid on a desert island after escaping from pirates. At first he lived on nothing but fruit. Then by chance, he met an English **castaway**. The man vanished into the jungle three days later. Luckily, he left behind several knives. Using these, Ashton could hunt tortoises for food. He was rescued by a ship soon after.

DESERT ISLAND
WHERE: often **tropical** but found all over the world
LARGEST: Devon Island, off northern Canada:
21,331 square miles (55,247 km²)

SURVIVING THE SURF

If your ship is sinking, you need to act quickly. Gather as much food and water as you can. If you do not have a life raft or **life jacket**, cling to something large that floats by. Kick slowly toward the island. Listen for the roar of the surf. The waves can push you to shore. Watch for razor-sharp **coral reefs** below the surface. They rip skin to shreds.

coral reef

CORAL REEF
WHERE: usually found along tropical coastlines
LARGEST: Great Barrier Reef, Australia: 1,600 miles (2,575 km) long

I SURVIVED

In 1943, a US ship was sunk by a Japanese destroyer. Braving sharks and crocodiles, the survivors swam to a nearby island. After two days without food and water, they swam to a bigger island. For six days, they survived on coconuts before being rescued. One of the survivors was John F. Kennedy, who later became the president of the United States.

If you make it to land, your chances of survival are much higher. It is easier to stay alive on an island than adrift at sea. If you take the right steps, you can build a **shelter**, find food and water, and make a fire for warmth, cooking, and protection.

waterfall

WATERFALL
USE: perfect for washing yourself and your clothing
THREAT: a sudden gush of water can sweep you away

OVER HERE!

If you are very lucky, you might find there are people already on the island. However, in the Pacific Ocean there are more than 30,000 islands and most have no one living on them. That is why they are called desert, or deserted, islands. You will need to do your best to attract attention and, hopefully, someone will rescue you.

SOS help signal

SOS DISTRESS SIGNAL
USE: international distress signal that is easy to type in **Morse code:** ··· — — — ···
THREAT: if written on a beach, watch for high tides

fire signal

TOUGH TIP

Use seaweed, rocks, or branches to spell out a message such as SOS or HELP. Leave your message in an open area. You can also use one of these well-known codes:

V = need help

X = need medical help

↑ = head this way

Shipping lanes crisscross the oceans. Passing ships and airplanes will probably pass your island at some point. The problem is letting rescuers know where you are. A smoky fire is the best way to attract attention. Build it on top of a hill or cliff, so that it can be seen from a long way away.

FIRE SIGNAL

INTERNATIONAL DISTRESS SIGNAL: three fires in a triangle

ADVANTAGE: easy to see from airplanes

LIGHTING A FIRE

A fire has many uses: as a signal, for cooking, and for light and warmth at night. The smoke also keeps insects away. To start a fire you need a material that catches light easily, called **tinder**. The "hair" from palm tree trunks works well. On top of the tinder, place the **kindling**. Then put lots of dead, dry palm leaves on top.

palm tree

PALM TREE
USE: green palm leaves create thick, white smoke when burned

TOUGH TIP

You can create fire by rubbing one piece of wood very fast against another. The wood gets very hot and sets the tinder on fire. Be warned, this is not very easy and takes a lot of skill and practice.

If you do not have matches or lighters, set fire to tinder by focusing the Sun's hot rays on it with a pair of glasses. Even the shiny bottom of a soda can will work! Practice until you can light your signal fire quickly, in case you see a ship or airplane passing by.

fire-making skills

FIRE-MAKING SKILLS
NEEDED: tinder, kindling, hard wooden pole, soft wooden board with notch for catching heated wood
ACTION: spin hard wooden pole to create a flame

11

WASHED UP

After a shipwreck, the remains of the ship and its **cargo** often get washed ashore. Look around the island for any washed-up garbage. Look out for items such as matches, a knife, a **compass**, a lighter, and a **first aid kit**. If your life raft has survived the trip ashore, you can use it as a shelter.

life raft

LIFE RAFT
WHAT: a boat used to get to safety
USE: often fitted with freshwater, food packets, fishing kit, a mirror, flares, and a first aid kit

12

Almost all cargo has some use. A plastic bag or bottle can be used to carry or store water. A short length of rope can help you trap animals or build a raft. A piece of wire can be bent and used to make a fish hook to catch fish.

TOUGH TIP

Dental floss can be used to make a clothes line or shoelaces, or to sew patches in your clothes.

SURVIVAL ESSENTIALS
WHAT: matches, compass, and knife
USE: matches to start a fire, compass to find your way, knife to cut and hunt

MAKING A SHELTER

Unless you come across a suitable cave, you will need to build your own shelter. First, find your materials. Bamboo is light and strong, and perfect for making a frame. Palm leaves provide excellent cover. Start with a simple **lean-to**. Plant two Y-shaped branches into the sand about 6 feet (1.8 m) apart. Take a long branch and place it between the forks. This creates a **ridgepole**.

driftwood

DRIFTWOOD
WHAT: wood washed ashore
USE: fire, shelter, or boat building

Lean more sticks or bamboo poles against the ridgepole to form a roof. Tie everything together with vines. You can also use lengths of bark from a hibiscus tree, which peels off like string. Place layers of palm leaves over your frame. To keep warm at night, line the floor with more palm leaves.

TOUGH TIP

Where should you build your shelter? Away from the beach, you have more protection from stormy weather and high tides. A shelter on the beach gives you a good view of the ocean, though. Choose carefully, your survival could depend on it.

shelter

SHELTER
MADE FROM: driftwood
USE: protects from Sun, wind, rain, and some animals

ANIMAL DANGER

Tropical islands may look like paradise, but they are home to some deadly creatures. Spiders and scorpions can give very serious bites. Though snakes are common on Pacific islands, only a few can harm you. If you do come across a snake, keep your distance. Crocodiles are a lot more dangerous. They are very fast over short distances, even out of water.

crocodile

CROCODILE
SIZE: grows up to 20 feet (6 m) long
THREAT: fast on land and in the water, powerful jaws, and sharp teeth

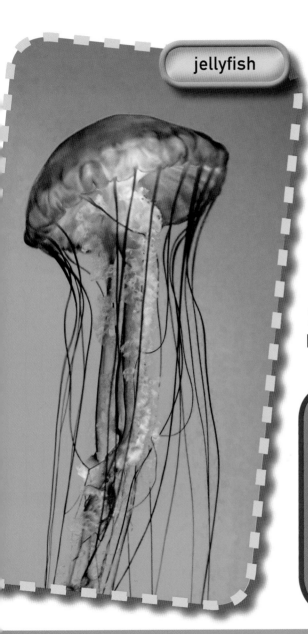

jellyfish

Watch out for box jellyfish. They have a very painful sting. Komodo dragons can grow up to 10 feet (3 m) long. These giant lizards have a bite so poisonous it can kill you. Even more deadly is the tiny cone snail. A drop of its poison can kill 20 people. Wear shoes even in water so you don't get poked by any poisonous creatures!

TOUGH TIP

Tiger sharks are known to attack humans near to the shore. Remember, they are most active at dawn and dusk. Get out of the water if you are bleeding because blood can attract sharks.

JELLYFISH
SWARM: up to 100,000 jellyfish in a large bloom (group)
THREATS: many have a painful sting

FOOD AND WATER

You can live for two weeks without food but only three to four days without freshwater. If you cannot find a stream, use large leaves to **funnel** rainwater into empty coconut shells. The next best thing is to drink coconut milk. Climb the tree and twist the nut until it breaks free.

coconut tree

TOUGH TIP

Never stand under a coconut tree and shake it to get coconuts. Every year people die from coconuts landing on their head!

COCONUT TREE
SIZE: up to 100 feet (30 m) tall
USE: young, green coconuts contain lots of vitamins and minerals

wild pigs

Wild pigs are found on many Pacific islands, but it is a real challenge to catch them. Birds are much easier to catch. Find out where they nest and feed. Then trap them with a **snare** made from a loop of string or a shoelace. Birds' eggs make a great meal, though gulls will attack anyone who comes near their nests. Frogs, snakes, and large bugs can all be eaten, too.

WILD PIGS
USE: can be eaten for food. Skin can be used for clothes.
THREAT: sharp tusks make them very dangerous if threatened

SEAFOOD DINNER

Along with coconuts and fruit, fish are your best bet for a meal. Bend a safety pin to make a fish hook, or sharpen a bamboo stick to make a spear. If you are a good swimmer, try diving underwater. If not, wade into knee-deep water. The water may distort the distance between you and the fish, so aim your throw around 6 inches (15 cm) ahead of your target. Try spearing the fish against a hard surface, such as a rock.

land crab

LAND CRAB
WHERE: found on most tropical islands
USE: meat in crab claws tastes good when cooked

Make yourself an underground oven to cook your catch. Dig yourself a hole in the ground. Then line it with hot rocks heated in your fire. Wrap the fish in palm leaves to keep it clean and moist. Put the wrapped fish on top of the rocks, cover it all with sand, and leave to cook.

filefish

FILEFISH
SIZE: up to 43 inches (1 m) long
USE: can be roasted and eaten

ISLAND WEAR

A tropical island is very hot. This is great for a summer vacation, but deadly on a desert island. Even on a cloudy day, the Sun will burn your skin in 15 minutes. Avoid the midday Sun, as **sunstroke** can be a killer. Stay in the shade as much as possible and always cover your head.

Avoid midday Sun.

MIDDAY SUN
TEMPERATURE: 80 to 90° F (27 to 32° C)
THREAT: Sun beats down for 10 hours or more on tropical islands

palm leaves

I SURVIVED

In the 1830s a woman named Juana Maria was stranded on an island off the coast of California. She lived alone for 18 years, wearing dresses made from bird skins sewn together. Her shelter was made from whale bones.

Most clothes today are not built for life on a desert island. You will have plenty of time, so learn how to make new clothes from palm leaves and coconut shells.

PALM LEAVES
LENGTH: up to 12 feet (3.6 m) long
USE: leaves can be woven to make baskets, mats, sacks, fans, and hats

EXPLORE!

At some point you will probably want to explore your island. You might find a better place to fish or to set up your shelter. But many Pacific islands are rocky and mountainous, and fast-flowing rivers can sweep you off your feet. You can get stuck in swamps and **quicksand**. Leave markers to show the route back to your shelter.

high ground

HIGH GROUND
USE: a good view of your island
THREATS: falling rocks, slippery surfaces, cliffs, and smoky volcanoes

freshwater

TOUGH TIP

Watch out for the Sun as you wander around. Rub coconut oil, a natural suntan lotion, onto your skin. Even better is the sticky ooze from a mushroom coral. This works like SPF 50 sunblock. Put the coral back in the sea and you can use it again the next day!

If you have a pen and paper, make a map of your island. Mark on it good places to find freshwater, fruit trees, or even waterfalls where you can take a shower. Spend a few days on the other side of the island, just in case ships pass by on that side.

FRESHWATER
WHERE: in ponds, rivers, lakes, ice, snow, and under the ground
THREAT: can contain bugs and diseases

FEELING LONELY

I t can get lonely on an island all by yourself. The important thing is to stay calm and think clearly. The ocean may separate you from civilization, but it is likely that a ship will pass by and rescue you. Make plans or scratch a mark on a tree as each day passes to keep up your spirits.

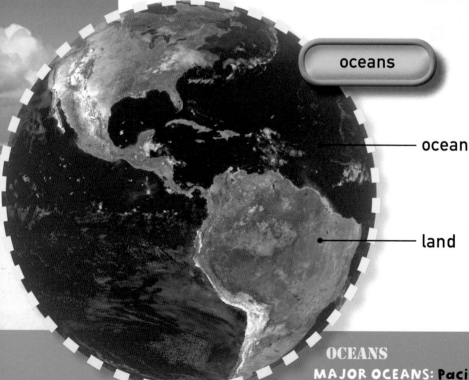

oceans

ocean

land

OCEANS
MAJOR OCEANS: Pacific, Atlantic, Indian, Arctic, and Southern
SIZE: 70 percent of the world is covered by ocean

Alexander Selkirk

These days, most castaways are eventually rescued. One man was stranded on an island during the 2004 **tsunami** in the Indian Ocean. He was found 25 days later, waving a flag made from some of his clothes. Even if you are not rescued within a few days, do not give up hope. Help is probably on its way.

I SURVIVED

In 1704, Scottish sailor Alexander Selkirk was **marooned** on an island in the middle of the Pacific. At first he read his Bible and waited to be rescued. When this did not happen, he made the best of life on the island. He hunted goats for food and built two huts out of wood. Finally, five years later, he was rescued.

ALEXANDER SELKIRK
TOOLS: musket, gunpowder, carpenter's tools, a knife, a Bible, some clothing, and rope
THREATS: sea lions, rats, and Spanish sailors (his enemies)

RESCUE

Most castaways are faced with a tough choice, to either stay on their island or take their chances on the ocean. Most desert islands have the materials to build a raft. Bamboo is the best material. It is light and strong, and floats well. You can make a sail by weaving palm leaves together and tying them to another bamboo frame.

bamboo raft

BAMBOO
SIZE: 45 feet (14 m) long
USES: medicines, shelter, furniture, paper, flutes, and fishing rods. Young shoots can be eaten.

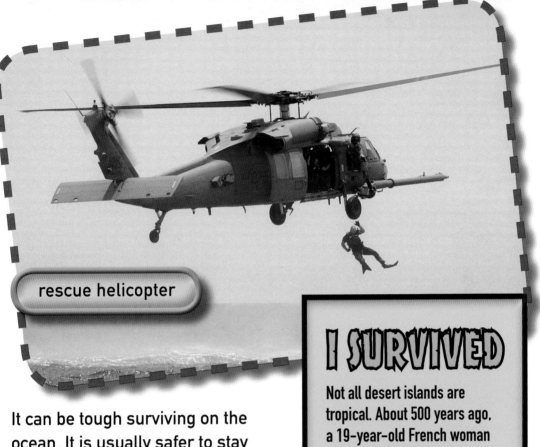

rescue helicopter

It can be tough surviving on the ocean. It is usually safer to stay on your island if you have a good supply of food and water. One day a passing ship or airplane will see the smoke from your signal fire, and you will be rescued. Some survivors have liked their desert island so much they decided to stay!

I SURVIVED

Not all desert islands are tropical. About 500 years ago, a 19-year-old French woman named Marguerite de La Rocque was marooned on an island off the coast of Canada. She survived by hunting wild animals. She lived in a cave for two years until a fishing boat finally rescued her.

RESCUE HELICOPTER
TYPE: Sikorsky HH-60 Pave Hawk
SPEED AND RANGE: 195 knots or 224 miles per hour (360 km/h); range of 500 miles (805 km)

GLOSSARY

cargo (KAHR-goh) Objects carried by a ship or plane.

castaway (KAST-uh-way) Someone who is adrift or shipwrecked.

compass (KUM-pus) A device that points towards North and can be used to find your way.

coral reefs (KOR-ul REEFS) Rock-like structures built by tiny ocean animals.

first aid kit (FURST AYD KIT) A box filled with medicines and bandages.

funnel (FUH-nul) To pour liquid into an object that is wide at one end and narrow at the other.

kindling (KIND-ling) Material that catches fire easily, such as small, dry sticks of wood.

lean-to (LEEN-too) A shelter made by leaning material such as wood against something.

life jacket (LYF JA-ket) A jacket filled with air that helps you to float in the water.

marooned (muh-ROOND) Left shore on a desert island.

Morse code (MORS KOHD) Signaling code made of dots and dashes.

quicksand (KWIK-sand) A deep pit filled with sand and water that can suck you in.

ridgepole (RIJ-pohl) A long pole at the top of a tent or shelter.

shelter (SHEL-ter) A structure that protects you.

shipwreck (SHIP-rek) When a ship sinks in a storm.

snare (SNAYR) A trap.

sunstroke (SUN-strohk) An illness that can kill you, which is caused by too much Sun.

tinder (TIHN-der) A material that easily bursts into flames.

tropical (TRAH-puh-kul) Hot, wet regions midway between the North and South Poles.

tsunami (soo-NAH-mee) A giant wave caused by an underwater earthquake.

FURTHER READING

Hodge, Susie. *Ocean Survival.* Extreme Habitats. New York: Gareth
   Stevens, 2008.

Llewellyn, Claire. *Survive on a Desert Island.* Survival Challenge. Charlotte, NC:
   Silver Dolphin Books, 2006.

MacAulay, Kelley, and Bobbie Kalman. *Tropical Oceans.* New York: Crabtree
   Publishing Company, 2006.

O'Shei, Tim. *How to Survive on a Deserted Island.* Prepare to Survive.
   Mankato, MN: Edge Books, 2009.

WEBSITES

Due to the changing nature of Internet links, PowerKids Press has
developed an online list of websites related to the subject of this book.
This site is updated regularly. Please use this link to access the list:
www.powerkidslinks.com/guide/island/

INDEX